# BARCLAY BUTERA

© 2008 Assouline Publishing
601 West 26th Street, 18th floor
New York, NY 10001, USA
Tel.: 212 989-6810  Fax: 212 647-0005
www.assouline.com

ISBN: 978 2 75940 287 8

Text © Barclay Butera

Printed in Singapore

# BARCLAY BUTERA

ASSOULINE

# CONTENTS

# INTRODUCTION

When I begin working on an interior I always approach the project with one simple rule: "yours, mine, and ours." Upon meeting a new client, he or she will bring their own tastes and experiences with them, and I of course come with my own tastes and experiences. The key is to find the right synergy and combine these elements in a way that pleases everyone. Being an interior designer is almost like being a therapist for the home—you are interpreting a client's residence based on your own aesthetic, and educating them on how you believe their house should look and feel. As a designer you have access to a person's most intimate living spaces, and it is important to help them achieve the kind of living that is best for them and truly reflects who they are.

I am originally from northern California, but have lived in southern California for nearly 25 years. I would not be where I am today without my southern California background—I have found creative freedom here unlike anywhere else. Because there are so few rules here when it comes to interiors, working in southern California has given me the opportunity to express myself in a way that wouldn't be possible in any other place—and I have been incredibly fortunate to do so.

I grew up in a home where the living and dining rooms were only used on special occasions. My work is absolutely the antithesis of that. I believe a home should be used—all of

it: the living room should be lived in, the dining room dined in. Unified, livable spaces are the key to a harmonious home. I have been lucky enough to live in some pretty glamorous places, including Frank Sinatra's Twin Palms estate in the desert, Desi Arnaz Jr.'s Beverly Hills home, and a cottage Bette Davis owned by the sea. It is important for me to be able to enjoy every aspect of a house, and to live in it the way it deserves to be lived in—with lots of entertaining and inspired style. That is why I do what I do: that element of surprise, the unexpected is what makes a house unique.

I do not believe in furnishing an entire house all at once. It is a process that should happen slowly and organically. Collecting pieces over a period of time adds depth to a space. I personally love the stories behind things, behind collections. I fill my home with all the fantastic pieces I've gathered over the years: beautiful glassware, English silver, and organic textures, such as horn and shell. They have all come from different places, and each item has a history. These little details are what add personality and warmth to a home. I like to think of them as conversation pieces, they have a story to tell.

I am known for layering patterns upon patterns and textures upon textures, such as placing a leopard area rug on top of wall-to-wall carpeting, or mixing animal prints with toiles. I've been known to blend a British Colonial look with old Hollywood, Asian with Spanish Colonial, and antiques with contemporary art. This diversity is adaptable from client to client. I am inspired by everything I see: movies, travel, books, fashion, and magazines; the list goes on. I love to keep tear sheets of beautiful things I have seen and figure out ways to incorporate them into my work. In the past I have drawn inspiration from sources as varied as the chic Hôtel Costes in Paris and the colorful boardwalk of Venice Beach.

Because my inspiration spans so many styles and periods, I have categorized it into five separate themes: Beach, City, Desert, Mountain, and Town & Country. These themes can often be combined with each other. It is easy to take an element from one place and drop it into another, and I encourage people to do so. I have recently introduced a textiles line for Kravet Couture. And I have also launched my own home fragrance line, which is also divided into and inspired by these five key categories.

I am thrilled to be expanding my brand into all of these new areas, all the while making it more accessible to a greater variety of people. My future ventures will involve more commercial projects including hotels and multiunit residential design. My principal goal

it: the living room should be lived in, the dining room dined in. Unified, livable spaces are the key to a harmonious home. I have been lucky enough to live in some pretty glamorous places, including Frank Sinatra's Twin Palms estate in the desert, Desi Arnaz Jr.'s Beverly Hills home, and a cottage Bette Davis owned by the sea. It is important for me to be able to enjoy every aspect of a house, and to live in it the way it deserves to be lived in—with lots of entertaining and inspired style. That is why I do what I do: that element of surprise, the unexpected is what makes a house unique.

I do not believe in furnishing an entire house all at once. It is a process that should happen slowly and organically. Collecting pieces over a period of time adds depth to a space. I personally love the stories behind things, behind collections. I fill my home with all the fantastic pieces I've gathered over the years: beautiful glassware, English silver, and organic textures, such as horn and shell. They have all come from different places, and each item has a history. These little details are what add personality and warmth to a home. I like to think of them as conversation pieces, they have a story to tell.

I am known for layering patterns upon patterns and textures upon textures, such as placing a leopard area rug on top of wall-to-wall carpeting, or mixing animal prints with toiles. I've been known to blend a British Colonial look with old Hollywood, Asian with Spanish Colonial, and antiques with contemporary art. This diversity is adaptable from client to client. I am inspired by everything I see: movies, travel, books, fashion, and magazines; the list goes on. I love to keep tear sheets of beautiful things I have seen and figure out ways to incorporate them into my work. In the past I have drawn inspiration from sources as varied as the chic Hôtel Costes in Paris and the colorful boardwalk of Venice Beach.

Because my inspiration spans so many styles and periods, I have categorized it into five separate themes: Beach, City, Desert, Mountain, and Town & Country. These themes can often be combined with each other. It is easy to take an element from one place and drop it into another, and I encourage people to do so. I have recently introduced a textiles line for Kravet Couture. And I have also launched my own home fragrance line, which is also divided into and inspired by these five key categories.

I am thrilled to be expanding my brand into all of these new areas, all the while making it more accessible to a greater variety of people. My future ventures will involve more commercial projects including hotels and multiunit residential design. My principal goal has always been to create environments that I myself would want to live in. We all want a little bit of luxury in our lives, whether that comes from the kind of art we hang on the walls to the upholstery we choose. Designing a home should be fun and free of rules and regulations. I like to think of my aesthetic as livable luxury, which can mean different things to different people, as long as it is about making a home warm and comfortable. I continue to be a lifestyle designer and a strong believer in creating spaces with history and depth. When it comes to good design I think the most important tools to have are passion, generosity, and the willingness to push yourself to the next level.

I am a fashion designer for the home. In my mind, turning a home into a cozy, inspired retreat is tantamount to a fashion designer sending his or her latest looks down a runway. I always notice the details. To me, the cufflinks on a shirt are equivalent to the nailheads on a sofa or the tufts on a headboard. They add texture and personality to an item of clothing or a piece of furniture. I am a classic dresser; I seek out bespoke tailoring and haberdashery. I love three-piece suits, chunky silk ties and great pocket squares, and I bring that same discerning eye to my interiors. I apply fashion principles to home furnishings, and this is the way I prefer to approach home design, with an eye toward the fresh and current while maintaining a traditional and timeless aesthetic. I hope that you will enjoy my designs and interiors as much as I do.

# BEACH

For whatever we lose (like a you or a me)
it's always ourselves we find in the sea.

E. E. Cummings

When it comes to beach living, whether a home is in the Hamptons, on the East Coast, or overlooking Laguna Beach, in Orange County, California, the important thing is to design an intimate living space—even when I'm working on a grand scale. I think of it as creating a personalized escape, no matter how intimidating the space. This makes designing a large home seem much more manageable, rather than like an enormous and overwhelming structure. I use a lot of blue and white when I work on beach homes, in addition to more neutral, sand-inspired colors blended with jewel tones. Combining varying hues of blue adds depth to a space. I love the look of layering blue on blue: a hit of cobalt next to a soothing periwinkle, and vice versa. This creates contrast and tension yet still transitions nicely. Bringing in seashells and coral from the shoreline is a great way of adding personality to a home. In my own Newport Beach, California, home, I have groups of shells, starfish, and coral displayed on coffee and side tables and nestled at the bases of hurricane lamps.

I don't shy away from using wallpaper or various applications of stone, hardwood, or woven materials on the ceilings and walls of a beach home. I have even been known to cover walls with bamboo or raffia. I love bringing that rustic, seaside feeling to every aspect of a house, including the more unexpected places. Even my furniture combines textures: I have used raffia upholstery on

armchairs covered with pale blue paisley cushions, and I have integrated furniture made of natural materials like wicker and sea grass, coordinating them with linens from my own Kravet Couture fabric line. Dramatic touches, such as draping a striking fabric over an elegant four-poster bed, can also look spectacular in a beach home. Introducing the unexpected helps to blend disparate elements together in an unconventional manner.

In my Newport Beach home, I papered the living room with Ralph Lauren Home toile wallpaper. Adding a bamboo cabinet filled with artifacts from the ocean, a shell-encrusted mirror and chandelier, and nautical paintings completed the look. For a consistent effect throughout the house, I had the ebony hardwood floors stained dark. I love how they contrast with the sand outside—it was an unusual choice because the tendency is to make beach-house floors lighter, rather than darker. However, the darker floors ground the overall house, and they contrast beautifully with the lighter walls. I couldn't resist including my signature animal prints, so I placed a leopard-print rug of my own design on the floor and threw in animal touches elsewhere, such as a zebra-print ottoman next to a pair of large blue-and-white vases.

Even when working on a beach house, I embrace the mantra that there are no rules in interiors. The beach is meant to be an escape from quotidian life, so blending prints and patterns can prove to be a wonderful outlet. Batik fabrics combined with stripes or paisleys can really make a beach home come alive. For *House and Garden* magazine's Hampton Designer Showhouse, I created an entry hall that featured a custom-colored carpet inspired by a geometric David Hicks design—a vintage beach look, yet striking just the same. In my own beach house, I used a meander, or Greek key design, in some places, along with very simple, symmetrical patterns. I love the graphic look of basic black, pale blue, and white banding details. It contributes a refreshing, contemporary touch to a beach setting. Though my beach colors of choice tend to be traditional blues and whites, I love challenging the concept of a beach house. I like to think of my design approach as "beach house with a twist." Not everything needs to be nautical: Incorporating interesting and unpredictable pieces, such as an antique chinoiserie secretary, a heavy mahogany bed, or Chinese porcelain vases, adds character and eclecticism to a seaside escape. Of course not every beach house needs a blue-and-white palette. I created a beach home in which the color scheme was grounded in pinks, reds, and greens, with an overall floral motif. The bed in the master bedroom was made of bamboo and draped in green-and-red floral bedding. I also used bamboo rods in the windows. There are so many exciting options within this category, but above all, a beach home should be a relaxing escape that expresses its owner's personality—and triggers an emotional response.

# CITY

When you look at a city, it's like reading the hopes,
aspirations and pride of everyone who built it.

Hugh Newell Jacobsen

The city is about slick metropolitan living. Designing a city interior involves blending transitional styles together and making the most of limited space. I love taking a very small area and turning it into an exciting room. For example, the maid's quarters in my Beverly Hills home were extremely narrow. I chose transparent lamps for the nightstands because they take up less space, visually. I added a luxurious zebra-skin rug and striking black-and-white photographs from the classic Hollywood era and converted the space into a stylish little guest room.

When we think of city living, we think of chaos, excitement, noise, and hustle and bustle. I enjoy creating cozy, distinctive retreats where one can relax while still enjoying the active pace of city life. When I step onto the deck of my Beverly Hills house, I look out at the dazzling lights of Los Angeles, but I am completely surrounded by the quiet elegance of trees. The house is only three miles from the city center, and yet on that deck I could easily be a million miles away. The most remarkable feature of a loft I designed in San Diego is its sweeping terrace; it turns the entire place into a remote and delightful haven, nestled high above the city's mayhem.

Dividing a space is another approach that works well in city homes. In a single-room residential loft on Sunset Boulevard, in Los Angeles, I created separate areas and tied them together with the consistent use of black and white, chrome, and nickel. The application of recurring elements, such as white walls or a repeating wallpaper pattern, keeps small rooms from becoming claustrophobic. I incorporated various household elements as partitions; a countertop separates the kitchen from the living room, a curtain divides a bedroom. Another way of defining space is by using furniture, such as a bar or a table, preferably a piece that is finished on at least three sides. In the same Sunset Boulevard loft, I installed shutters in an area that had no windows to create the illusion of sunlight. I then painted the walls behind them blue for an added trompe l'oeil effect.

I also like including abstract oil paintings in city settings—pieces that express a strong sense of color and atmosphere. Photographs are another favorite detail; in my Beverly Hills home, I transferred small black-and-white photos onto Lucite panels and lit them from behind. I grouped them above a bed, as a collection can have a greater impact than one single piece. Those photographs, combined with bronze-filigree light fixtures and mirrored nightstands, create an eclectic bedroom reminiscent of Hollywood's golden age.

Another way to give a small city space greater impact is by layering art over brightly colored wallpaper. I like to think of wallpaper as a painter's canvas. My job as an interior designer is to add the punch that makes it distinctive. In that same Beverly Hills house, I used a lively wallpaper pattern called Woodstock, made by Cole & Son, that consists of deep tangerines and has a very groovy, psychedelic sixties vibe. I added abstract artwork and then a bed with a tufted headboard and nickel nailheads. I topped everything off with a few cushions in my signature animal print. The striking combination brings the small space to life, evoking the chic style and pizzazz of 1960s Hollywood.

Details are important, especially when it comes to tight city spaces. I once used a black-lacquered screen with an intricate Asian carving in the center as a makeshift window covering. I tend not to use very heavy drapery treatments, so introducing this unusual element was a good way of adding a touch of glamour to the window while also filtering the light.

I prefer natural or soft, dim light, rather than bright, overhead lighting. Overlighting a home is a mistake that a lot of people make. When you walk into a home you want to feel warmth and emotion. Residences I've worked on rely on great incandescent lighting such as table lamps and floor lamps. This type of light can be further enhanced by custom lampshades. Whether decoupaged, handpainted, or made of fabric in unique shapes, they add another element of good design to a room. A city dwelling should be an inviting refuge that radiates warmth, makes the most of limited space, and is as unique and fascinating as its owner.

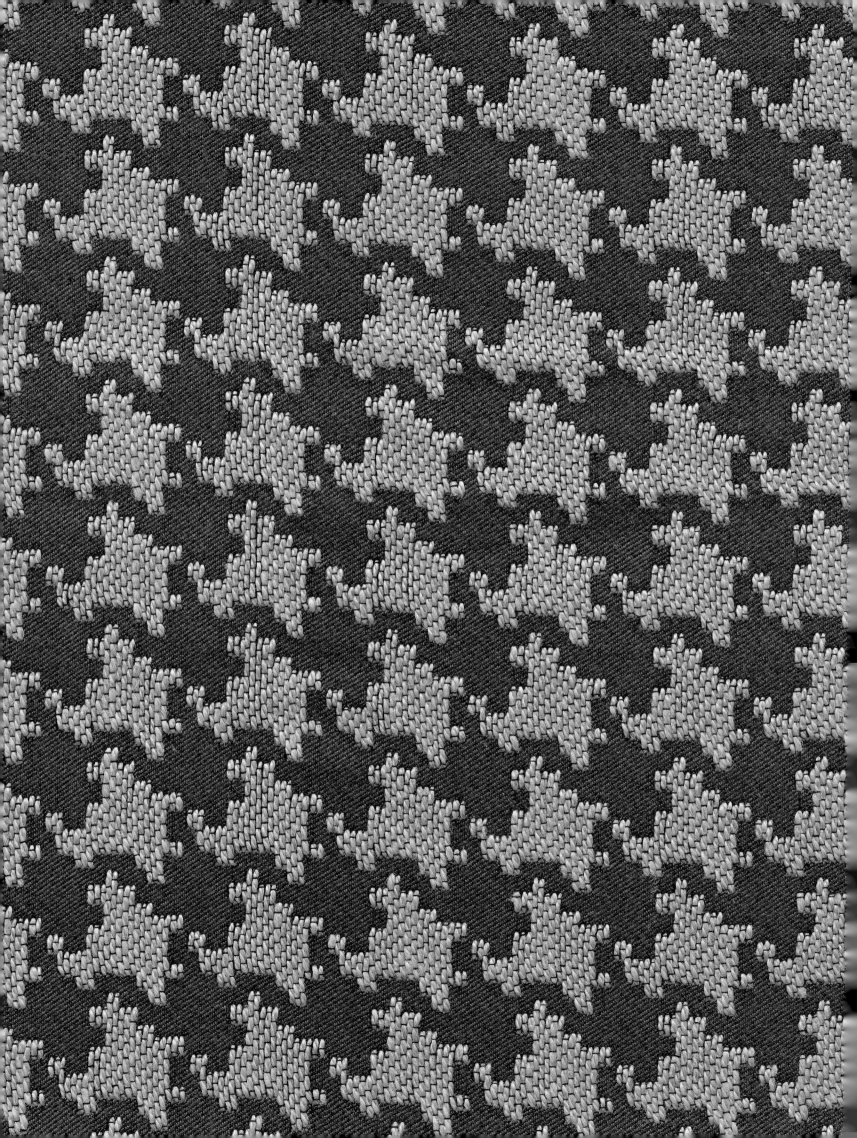

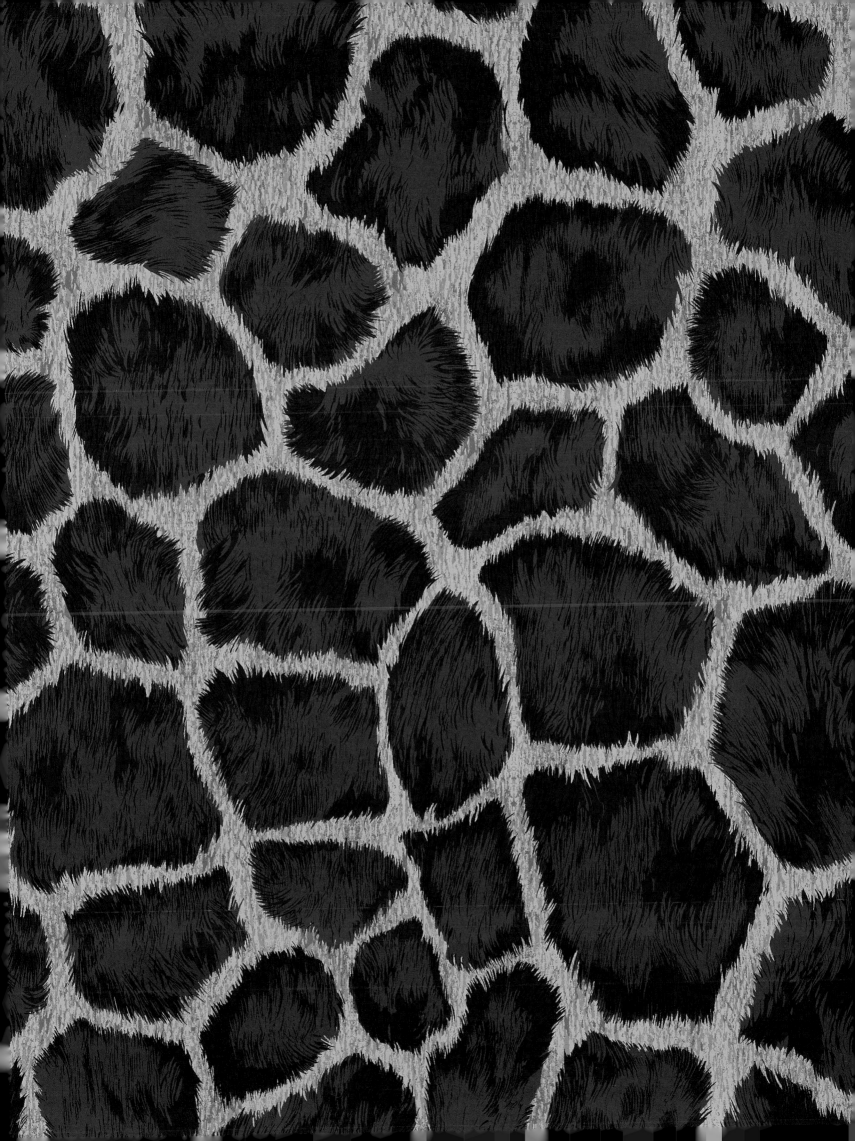

prints; the integration of earthy materials such as suede, linen, and natural silk; the inclusion of striking objets d'art, such as an old Indonesian wheel perched on an armoire next to an open gas-fire pit; and beautiful, carved beds made of mahogany. These are both traditional and untraditional elements that I love incorporating into a desert panorama, where the landscape can be so stark. There are, however, certain areas where I am always consistent in a desert setting. If I decide to use slate for the countertops, I will use slate throughout the home—on all the countertops in the kitchen and bathrooms. I am also consistent when it comes to wood trim, which helps to ground an interior by repeating a familiar theme.

I enjoy the creative process of figuring out what to do with an outdoor space. In my Palm Springs home, I installed a teak overhang so that I, along with my pet dachshunds, could enjoy a combination of indoor and outdoor living and dining. I draped airy white fabrics over large pieces of rattan furniture to create an exterior-lounge atmosphere. The stunning natural foliage is a huge part of that residence. My home in southern Utah is more remote, and the views are much more extreme than those in Palm Springs, so I wanted to reflect that in the interiors I created. The beauty of the house depends on natural light, and I installed seamless windows so the serenity of the austere desert environment can be enjoyed throughout; both the living room and master bedrooms also look out on those sublime panoramas. I used lots of deep reds and taupes and tried to assimilate the natural beauty of the outdoors into the interiors. I placed rush stems in planters and shadow boxes and hung lithographs of trees over the bed. The furniture is a mixture of wood and wicker, with a few standout pieces such as a zebra chair I found in Paris.

I paired the striking animal-print chair with a unique desk with a log base and a leather top. Contemporary art is displayed throughout, and leather and animal-hide pillows add exotic accents. I recently introduced eco-friendly inserts to my pillow collections. They are now filled with feathers and corn by-products. The inner covers are made of unbleached cotton and are biodegradable, which perfectly complements this naturalistic setting. In the living room, I mixed and matched upholstery patterns—from a houndstooth check to paisley to animal prints.

While a desert home is very much about the surrounding environment, it's important to remember that the desert aesthetic is not necessarily limited to desert locations. It is entirely possible to take a desert-inspired idea, such as a cowhide pillow, and drop it into a mountain retreat or a city home. And a beach, town-and-country, mountain, or city motif can likewise add surprising and refreshing detail to a desert residence. In one way or another, my five categories overlap and cross-pollinate.

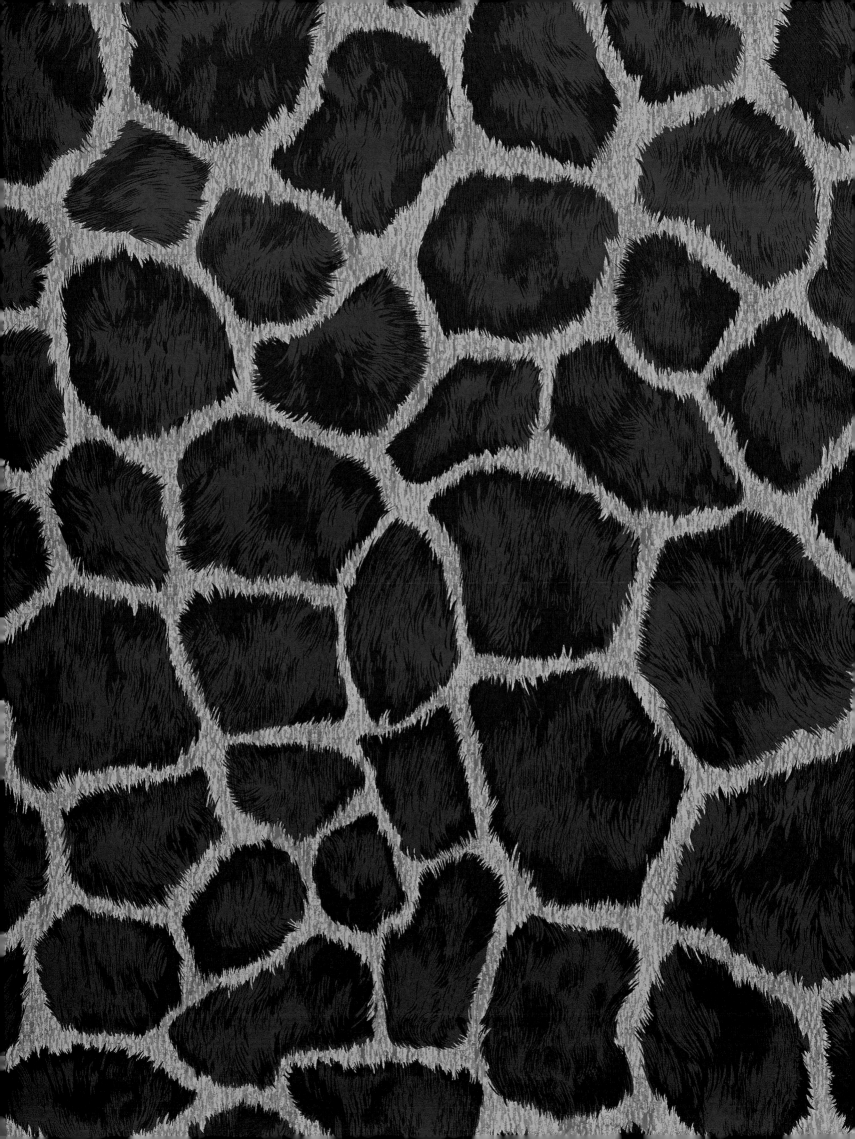

# MOUNTAIN

Mountains have a dreamy way of folding up a noisy day
in quiet covers, cool and gray.

Leigh Buckner Hanes

When it comes to alpine lodges or chalets, I pay very close attention to the wood detailing, whether it is on the ceiling, wainscoting, crown moldings, or baseboards. I love to add that all-important finishing touch at the precise point where the wall meets the ceiling or the floor. Close attention to detail adds coherence to a home and ties the whole look together. I installed a beautiful, vaulted wood ceiling over the study of my mountain home. It adds a dramatic, almost cathedral-like touch to a cozy interior space. The moment you enter the room, you are instantly catapulted into a re-creation of a gentlemen's study or a private club from an earlier era. I put in a large game table surrounded by comfy leather chairs: It is the perfect place to chat with friends or fix yourself a cocktail. My showroom in Park City is also influenced by this theme. I recently debuted an "Out of Africa" collection, and some of the inspiration came from the stately gentlemen's club featured in the 1985 movie of the same name. Even though a snowcapped mountain is not exactly the Serengeti, there are a wide variety of colors and fabrics that could overlap in both settings. What I love about my five design categories is the way they are all able to intersect fluidly with one another.

Leather is one of my favorite materials, especially when I'm designing a home in a mountain setting. I used it on the furniture throughout my own house, on rustic wicker and bamboo chairs,

and on a sofa studded with nailheads. I also chose a chunky leather bed topped with plaid and paisley cushions for the master bedroom. I covered other pieces in corduroy and chenille.

Landscape oil paintings also add to the gentlemen's-club atmosphere. I also love to hang oils featuring stags, roosters, and other scenes of animals and nature. Unlike a metropolitan city setting, where modern abstract art works best, I find that romantic or realist paintings fit in well in an alpine context and help to draw you into the environment. As in my four other design categories, I'm a big fan of texture and layering in a mountain setting. I'll throw patterned area rugs over a slate floor and put in some bucolic log chairs with red-plaid backs. Every available surface is covered with a textured rug, a cushion, or a throw. My color palette tends to showcase deep cranberries, vivid rusts, rich chocolates, and lush velvets. Those are the shades I associate with a mountain panorama. The seating areas are all accented with the occasional decoupaged or gesso-glazed lampshade. I see these details as an essential part of the collection of a well-traveled gentleman.

My house offers sweeping views of the surrounding mountains, and it is wonderful to be reminded of where you are simply by looking out a window. As with a desert home, scenery is everything in the alpine setting. Another way to achieve the chalet aesthetic—even if you don't live at the foot of a mountain—is by turning a room into a log cabin. Here again we see the importance of wood detailing; the logs on the walls and ceilings add warmth and ambience and immediately pull you into a snug and inviting space. No matter how large a dwelling is, it's important to avoid a grand-scale home feeling and to make the interiors comfortable and homey. I love to add quirky details such as alternating dining chairs: One leather armchair next to a plaid side chair, for example, is much more visually interesting than identical chairs, side by side. A mountain home is more about comfort and less about formality, so it is much easier to get away with such departures from convention.

Mounting trophy antlers, horn pieces, or other taxidermic items on the walls is another way to achieve a lodgelike aura. These can function as conversation pieces or simply as whimsical items to make guests grin. Inserting one grounding piece of furniture into a room is sometimes all it takes to get people talking. For example, an oversize chest of drawers placed in the living room instead of the bedroom can be a great place to store magazines or board games. The key is to highlight those spectacular pieces of furniture and to not be afraid of mixing styles. Bold and unusual choices add sophistication to an alpine lodge, which is exactly the way I like it—a cozy interior that reflects the grandiosity and stateliness of the surrounding mountains.

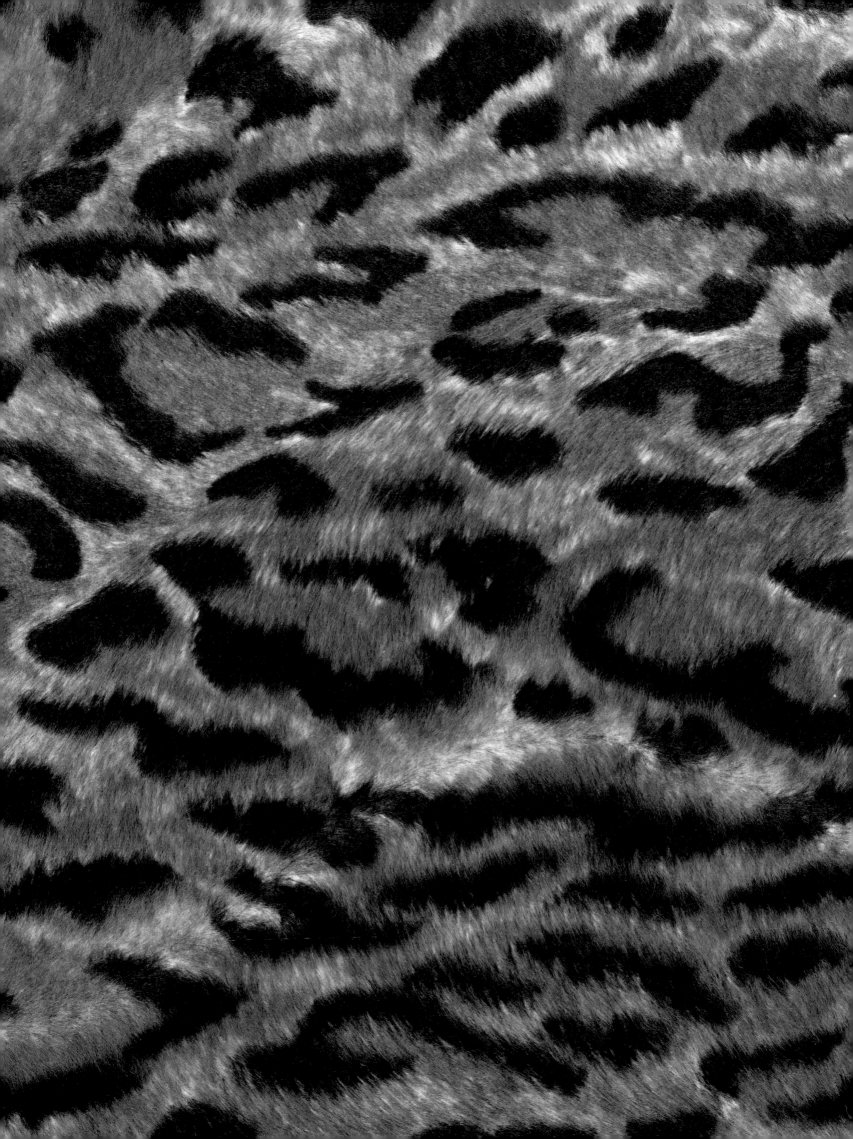

# TOWN AND COUNTRY

It is not easy to walk alone in the country
without musing upon something.

Charles Dickens

When I think of town and country, I picture elegant, stately manor houses in cities such as Greenwich, Connecticut, and Atlanta, Georgia, or any other place that exhibits a high level of good taste. This look is about chic suburban homes that serve as primary residences.

Accessories are key when it comes to a town-and-country interior. This is why I like to install bookcases in these environments: When people travel, they bring back artifacts such as antique boxes, clock faces, silver, native art, or ceremonial objects. These items should be proudly displayed on shelves or in curio cabinets for guests to enjoy. Such mementos are there to tell stories; they provide visitors to a home with fascinating information about who its owners are, what they like, and where they have been. I find that there is a lot of history and memory associated with the town-and-country home.

There are endless possibilities for decorating a town-and-country residence: Rich paisley wallpaper can provide a wonderful backdrop to an equestrian oil painting. Leopard-print throw pillows can be paired with vibrant plaid bedding. Window treatments can be more elaborate than in a desert or a beach home, and when it comes to fabrics, it is fun to combine staid stripes with vivid florals. Both are classic town-and-country motifs. I also love incorporating seemingly incongruous details. I once located a set of antlers at an old estate in England and hung them over the mantelpiece of a California home. I then placed a pair of blue-and-white Ming dynasty–era vases on top of a simple coffee table by the mantel for an eclectic effect. Notable details like a heavy iron chandelier or a cobalt blue lamp can also be added to the mix.

I recently launched a Regency Collection inspired by Paris in the 1920s. I visited numerous Parisian hotels and cafés and created a very tailored, fashion-inspired look: chartreuse trim with gold and silver leaf accents, lots of deep currants, and jewel tones. I use a lot of saturated color in this category, and I could easily picture one of my chairs—such as the Wyland Wing Chair, with its rounded back, oversize nailhead, and carved-bracket base—in a town-and-country living room.

Without the lure of big-city attractions close by, people tend to spend a lot of their leisure time in these homes, and it is important to make all the rooms amenable to relaxation. A master bedroom can truly become a retreat; elegant beamed arches, a four-poster, and a separate living area are all features that, to me, invoke livable luxury. Lush greenery is also extremely important to a town-and-country house: potted plants and freshly cut flowers make a residence much friendlier and more enjoyable.

I once designed the interiors of a bayfront home in the Southeast for *House Beautiful* magazine. Despite the location, I considered it to be a town-and-country home, rather than a city dwelling or a seaside cottage. I tried to include elements of Palm Beach, Florida, and blend them into a spa-retreat theme. I used horn-framed mirrors, lots of black lacquer, and hues of eggplant and chocolate. I covered the walls with bamboo and used silk reeded wallpaper on the ceiling, which filled the house with warmth. I hung palm-leaf lithographs using transparent frames, so the matting was actually the bamboo background.

Even though this home could fit into a beach or city setting, I like to think of it as town-and-country because it is very much a retreat. The bedrooms and living rooms of a town-and-country home are meant to be inviting places where people can lounge after a day at work or on the weekends. The color scheme of this residence felt very town-and-country to me: tonal greens and subtle chocolates. I also added large floral pillows that reminded me of Palm Beach in the 1960s and put in a pair of striped slipper chairs for added comfort and style. I believe that it is possible to live this way anywhere; such design choices are not merely limited to suburban areas. Town and country is about comfort and elegance. It combines rich living, country casual, and generational residences. This lifestyle is as much about living as it is about entertaining. It represents lineage and heritage, family and friends, dogs and children, and it transcends the changing of the seasons.

# CREDITS

Andrew Abrecht Photography, pages 49, 52-54

www.abrechtphotography.com


Danny Lee Photography

C&S Homes Inc, pages 96-99, 102-103

www.dleephotography.com

www.candshomesinc.com


Look Photography, pages 10-13, 35, 60-62, 74-83, 162-165

www.lookphotogpraphy.com


Lori Brystan Photography, Barclay Butera Headshots

www.brystan-studios.com


Mark Lohman, pages 15-33, 36-37, 43, 50-51, 66-71, 85-95, 105-107, 110-126, 128-131,

134-141, 146-160, 166-171

www.marklohmanphoto.com


Miguel Flores-Vianna, pages 44-45, 64-65

www.floresvianna.com


Scot Zimmerman, pages 100, 127, 133, 142-143

www.scotzimmermanphotography.com


Barclay Butera Inc. Photography, pages 40, 46-47, 56-58, 174

www.barclaybutera.com


Fabrics all from Barclay Butera Home and Kravet Showrooms

# ACKNOWLEDGMENTS

Having grown up in the interiors industry with my mother, Karen Butera, I learned from a young age the value of hard work and integrity. My father, Richard Butera, was an great example of the entrepreneurial spirit and taught me to always go after my dreams. Together they pushed me to reach for more in everything I did. Educated in Political Science and Economics with a year in law school, I developed a grounded knowledge in business. The combination of my education and the creativity I was exposed to from years in the family interior design business, set the foundation for the development of my own business.

When I was selecting a team 14 years ago that would grow and showcase the direction in which I was heading, I met Ray Langhammer. Together we created shopping environments that are nationally recognized and noted as a model for retailing by top manufacturers throughout the home furnishings industry. I credit Ray for his strong creative talent and drive in helping create the synergy between my two companies: Barclay Butera Inc and Barclay Butera Home both of which both continue to garner strong national support and exposure.

Beginning with two employees in 1994 and currently employing over one hundred, I have yet to be satisfied. Looking towards the future, each season is a new beginning, a chance to exceed your previous accomplishments.

My passion is a compounded goal, always pushing myself to the next plateau.

A special thanks to Elizabeth Blair Quinn, to Assouline for making this book possible and to the entire Kravet Family and their incredible staff's dedication in developing my new fabric collection.

Thank you to all my family, friends and dedicated staff who have helped and guided me along the way!